80% Python Minutes

By Weiran Ye

To Jinzi, Arthur, Adam, and Max for their support!

```
>>> # after being a programmer for many years,
... # when I started to use Python,
... # I wish there was a Python book that
... # - does not try to sell me Python
... # - does not explain what a for loop is
... # - does not have 300 pages
... # instead, a Python book that
... # - shows the first 80% of Python "things" that I
should know
... # - in 20 minutes
... # - with examples, A LOT OF examples
... # - and where are the land mines if I came from
other languages.
... #
... # if that resonates with you, this book is for
you!
... #
... # here we go
...
>>>
>>> x = 1
>>> x
1
>>> y = 2
>>> x + y
3
>>> type(x)
<class 'int'>
>>> # this is a Python comment
...
>>> # you can use exit() to quit the Python
interpreter.
... exit()
```

```
>>> a = 'this is a string'
>>> a
'this is a string'
>>> b = "double quotes work too"
>>> b
'double quotes work too'
>>> type(b)
<class 'str'>
>>> a + b
'this is a stringdouble quotes work too'
>>> x = 1
>>> x + b      # an int plus a str will fail
Traceback (most recent call last):
 File "<stdin>", line 1, in <module>
TypeError: unsupported operand type(s) for +: 'int'
and 'str'
>>> str(x) + b     # need to explicitly convert type
'1double quotes work too'


>>> type(b)
<class 'str'>
>>> b = 3     # Python is a dynamically-typed
language. b was a str
>>> b
3
>>> type(b)     # now it is an int
<class 'int'>


>>> p = 3.14
```

```
>>> type(p)
<class 'float'>
>>> r = float("1.23")
>>> type(r)
<class 'float'>
>>> s = float("some str")
Traceback (most recent call last):
 File "<stdin>", line 1, in <module>
ValueError: could not convert string to float: 'some
str'


>>> t = True
>>> type(t)
<class 'bool'>
>>> f = not t
>>> f
False
>>> t and f
False
>>> t or f
True
>>> t or False
True


>>> number_one = 1234
>>> number_2 = 1234
>>> numberThree = 1234
>>> _some_internal_var = 1234
>>> 4_number = 1234    # var name cannot start with
digits
  File "<stdin>", line 1
```

```
SyntaxError: invalid decimal literal
>>> and = 1234    # var name cannot be keywords
  File "<stdin>", line 1
    and = 1234    # var name cannot be keywords
    ^
SyntaxError: invalid syntax


>>> t1 = (1, 2, 3)    # this is a tuple
>>> type(t1)
<class 'tuple'>
>>> t2 = 4, 5, 6    # also a tuple with only commas
>>> type(t2)
<class 'tuple'>
>>> t1[0]    # index is zero-based
1
>>> t1[1]
2
>>> t3 = ('hello', 123, 4.56)    # tuple can store
different types
>>> t3[0]
'hello'
>>> t3[0] = 'world'    # attempt to update element in
a tuple, but...
Traceback (most recent call last):
  File "<stdin>", line 1, in <module>
TypeError: 'tuple' object does not support item
assignment
>>> # tuple is immutable, means it cannot be modified
...


>>> list1 = ['hello', 123, 4.56]    # this is a list
```

```
>>> list1[0]
'hello'
>>> list1[0] = 'world'     # list is mutable
>>> list1
['world', 123, 4.56]
>>> # why use tuples over lists then?
... # 1) if you don't want to (accidentally) modify
the elements
... # 2) tuples have better performance
...


>>> person = {'name':'John', 'age':35,
'employed':True}
>>> # that is a dictionary (dict)
>>> type(person)
<class 'dict'>
>>> person['name']
'John'
>>> person['name'] = 'Joe'
>>> person['name']
'Joe'


>>> colors = {'red','green','blue'}     # this is a
set
>>> colors
{'green', 'red', 'blue'}
>>> type(colors)
<class 'set'>
>>> duplicate_colors = {'red','red','green','blue'}
>>> duplicate_colors     # all elements are unique in
a set
```

```
    {'green', 'red', 'blue'}


>>> # tuple/list/dict/set are all container types.
... # let's see some common operations for all of
them.
...
>>> my_tuple = (1, 2, 3, 4, 5, 6, 7)
>>> my_list = [1, 2, 3, 4, 5, 6, 7]
>>> my_dict = {'name':'John', 'age':35,
'employed':True}
>>> my_set = {1, 2, 3, 4, 5, 6, 7}


>>> # size?
...
>>> len(my_tuple)
7
>>> len(my_list)
7
>>> len(my_dict)
3
>>> len(my_set)
7


>>> # min, max?
...
>>> min(my_tuple)
1
>>> min(my_list)
1
>>> min(my_dict)      # dicts sort by keys, not values
```

```
'age'
>>> min(my_set)
1


>>> # index?
...
>>> my_tuple[1]
2
>>> my_list[1]
2
>>> my_dict[1]    # dicts don't have index, use key
to get value
Traceback (most recent call last):
 File "<stdin>", line 1, in <module>
KeyError: 1
>>> my_dict['age']
35
>>> my_set[1]    # sets are not ordered, no index
Traceback (most recent call last):
 File "<stdin>", line 1, in <module>
TypeError: 'set' object is not subscriptable


>>> # index on steroids
...
>>> my_tuple[2:4]    # index 2 to 4, excluding 4
(3, 4)
>>> my_tuple[2:]    # from index 2 to the end
(3, 4, 5, 6, 7)
>>> my_tuple[:4]    # up to index 4, excluding 4
(1, 2, 3, 4)
>>> my_tuple[:]    # everything
```

```
(1, 2, 3, 4, 5, 6, 7)
>>> my_tuple[-1]    # first one but counting backward
7
>>> my_tuple[:-1]    # up to first one but counting
backward, excluding
(1, 2, 3, 4, 5, 6)
>>> my_tuple[::2]    # everything but skip by 2
positions, i.e., step=2
(1, 3, 5, 7)


>>> # check existence
...
>>> 3 in my_tuple
True
>>> 13 in my_tuple
False
>>> 3 in my_list
True
>>> 'age' in my_dict    # for dict, 'in' checks keys,
not values
True
>>> 35 in my_dict
False
>>> 3 in my_set
True


>>> # append new element, then remove it
>>> # tuple is immutable, no append
...
>>> my_list.append(8)
>>> my_list
```

```
[1, 2, 3, 4, 5, 6, 7, 8]
>>> my_list.pop()
8
>>> my_list
[1, 2, 3, 4, 5, 6, 7]
>>> my_dict['sex'] = 'male'     # add new key/value
>>> my_dict
{'name': 'John', 'age': 35, 'employed': True, 'sex':
'male'}
>>> my_dict.pop('sex')
'male'
>>> my_dict
{'name': 'John', 'age': 35, 'employed': True}
>>> my_set.add(8)
>>> my_set
{1, 2, 3, 4, 5, 6, 7, 8}
>>> my_set.remove(8)
>>> my_set
{1, 2, 3, 4, 5, 6, 7}


>>> # insertion by index
... # tuple is immutable, no insertion
... # dict and set are unordered, no insertion by
index.
...
>>> my_list.insert(0, 100)
>>> my_list
[100, 1, 2, 3, 4, 5, 6, 7]
>>> my_list.pop(0)
100
```

```
>>> # remove a value.
>>> # tuple is immutable, no removal
>>> # removing specific value from a dict is not
common, skip
...
>>> my_list.remove(3)
>>> my_list
[1, 2, 4, 5, 6, 7]
>>> my_set.remove(3)
>>> my_set
{1, 2, 4, 5, 6, 7}


>>> # clear all
... # tuple is immutable, cannot clear
...
>>> my_list.clear()
>>> my_list
[]
>>> my_dict.clear()
>>> my_dict
{}
>>> my_set.clear()
>>> my_set
set()


>>> # set operations
...
>>> set1 = {1,2,3,4}
>>> set2 = {3,4,5,6}
>>> set1 | set2
{1, 2, 3, 4, 5, 6}
```

```
>>> set1 & set2
{3, 4}
>>> set1 - set2
{1, 2}
>>> set1 ^ set2
{1, 2, 5, 6}
>>> set1 < set2    # subset
False
>>> set3 = {1,2,3,4,5}
>>> set1 < set3
True


>>> # when to use what?
>>> # if need set operation -> set
>>> # else if key/value pairs -> dict
>>> # else if needs performance and/or readonly ->
tuple
>>> # else -> list
...


>>> my_str = 'the quick brown fox jumps over the lazy
dog'
>>> myStr[0]    # str is just ordered sequence of
chars. str is immutable.
't'
>>> len(my_str)
43
>>> 'a' in my_str
True
>>> 'A' in my_str
False
```

```
>>> 'lazy' in my_str
True
>>> 'busy' in my_str
False
>>> my_str = my_str + '!'
>>> my_str
'the quick brown fox jumps over the lazy dog!'
>>> my_str += '?'
>>> my_str
'the quick brown fox jumps over the lazy dog!?'
>>> my_str = my_str[:-1]
>>> my_str
'the quick brown fox jumps over the lazy dog!'
>>> my_str = my_str[:-1]
>>> my_str
'the quick brown fox jumps over the lazy dog'
>>> my_str.split()
['the', 'quick', 'brown', 'fox', 'jumps', 'over',
'the', 'lazy', 'dog']
>>> my_str.split('j')
['the quick brown fox ', 'umps over the lazy dog']
>>> my_str.startswith('a')
False
>>> my_str.startswith('t')
True
>>> my_str.endswith('z')
False
>>> my_str.endswith('g')
True
>>> my_str.count(' ')
8
>>> my_str.upper()
'THE QUICK BROWN FOX JUMPS OVER THE LAZY DOG'
```

```
>>> my_str.capitalize()
'The quick brown fox jumps over the lazy dog'
>>> my_str.title()
'The Quick Brown Fox Jumps Over The Lazy Dog'
>>> # TIPS: always remember str is immutable,
>>> # so don't try to change it, instead,
>>> # think about assigning changes back to a new
variable
...


>>> # type conversions
...
>>> int('123')    # str -> int
123
>>> int(1.23)     # float -> int, truncate
1
>>> int(-1.23)
-1
>>> str(123)      # int -> str
'123'
>>> str(1.23)     # float -> str
'1.23'
>>> str(True)     # bool -> str
'True'
>>> float('1.23')    # str -> float
1.23
>>> float(123)      # int -> float
123.0
>>> bool(0)     # int -> bool, 0 is False; otherwise,
True
False
>>> bool(123)
```

```
True
>>> bool(-1)
True
>>> bool('')      # str -> bool, empty string is False;
otherwise, True
False
>>> bool('abc')
True
>>> bool('False')
True
>>> bool(0.0)     # float -> bool, 0.0 is False,
otherwise, True
False
>>> bool(0.1)
True
>>> tuple([1,2,3])     # list -> tuple
(1, 2, 3)
>>> # dict -> tuple. only takes keys.
... tuple({'name':'John', 'age':35, 'employed':True})
('name', 'age', 'employed')
>>> tuple({1,2,3})      # set -> tuple
(1, 2, 3)
>>> list((1,2,3))     # tuple -> list
[1, 2, 3]
>>> # dic -> list. only takes keys.
... list({'name':'John', 'age':35, 'employed':True})
['name', 'age', 'employed']
>>> list({1,2,3})
[1, 2, 3]
>>> list("abc")     # str --> list
['a', 'b', 'c']
>>> # list of tuples -> dict
```

```
... dict([('name','John'), ('age',35),
('employed',True)])
{'name': 'John', 'age': 35, 'employed': True}
>>> set((1,2,3))    # tuple -> set
{1, 2, 3}
>>> set([1,2,3])    # list -> set
{1, 2, 3}
>>> # dict -> set. only takes keys.
... set({'name':'John', 'age':35, 'employed':True})
{'age', 'name', 'employed'}


>>> # basic math
...
>>> 11 + 3
14
>>> 11 - 3
8
>>> 11 * 3
33
>>> 11 / 3
3.6666666666666665
>>> 11 // 3     # floor
3
>>> 11 % 3
2
>>> 11 ** 3
1331
>>> 1 + 2 * 3
7
>>> (1 + 2) * 3
9
>>> abs(-3)
```

```
3
>>> round(3.14159)
3
>>> round(3.14159, 4)
3.1416
>>> pow(11,3)
1331
>>> x = 11
>>> x += 3
>>> x
14


>>> # output
...
>>> print('this is an output')
this is an output
>>> print(123)
123
>>> x = 123
>>> print(x)
123
>>> print(x + 1)
124
>>> name = 'John'
>>> age = 35
>>> is_employed = True
>>> print(name,age,is_employed)    # spaces will be
added in between
John 35 True
>>> print(f'{name} is {age} years old.')    # called
f-strings, available python 3.6+
John is 35 years old.
```

```
>>> # input
...
>>> s = input("what is your name? ")
what is your name? John
>>> s
'John'
>>> s = input("How old are you? ")    # all inputs
are str, even entered a number
How old are you? 35
>>> s
'35'


>>> # 'if' condition
...
>>> percent = 70
>>> if percent < 25:     # ':' means expecting a new
block below
...     print('low')     # Python uses indent to
indicate block
... elif percent > 75:
...     print('high')
... else:
...     print('mid')
...
mid
>>> # other languages use curly braces, such as {
block_statements }
... # but Python uses ':' and indentations.
... # That makes Python code relatively more
readable.
```

```
...
>>> # conditional assignment
...
>>> output = 'more than half' if percent > 50 else
'not enough'
>>> output
'more than half'


>>> # while loop
...
>>> x = 0
>>> while x < 100:
...     if x == 1:
...         print('skipping 1, continue')
...         x += 1
...         continue
...     print(f'x={x}')
...     if x == 3:
...         print('reached 3, break')
...         break
...     x += 1
...
x=0
skipping 1, continue
x=2
x=3
reached 3, break


>>> # for loop
...
```

```
>>> rainbow =
['red','orange','yellow','green','blue','indigo','vio
let']
>>> for color in rainbow:
...     print(color)
...
red
orange
yellow
green
blue
indigo
violet
>>> for i in range(10):      # 0 to 10 (exclusive)
...     if i % 2 == 1:
...         continue
...     print(i)
...
0
2
4
6
8
>>> # similar to while loop, 'continue' and 'break'
can be used in for loop.
...


>>> # define and call a function
...
>>> def add_two_nums(x, y):     # again, use ':', not
{ }
...     return x + y
```

```
...
>>> sum = add_two_nums(3,7)
>>> sum
10
>>> # you may wonder, what if I pass in values other
than numbers?
...
>>> sum = add_two_nums(True, 'something')
Traceback (most recent call last):
 File "<stdin>", line 1, in <module>
 File "<stdin>", line 2, in add_two_nums
TypeError: unsupported operand type(s) for +: 'bool'
and 'str'
>>> # you may want to do data type validation.
... # but hold on to that, a more pythonic way is
EAFP.
... # EAFP stands for "easier to ask for forgiveness
than permission".
... # it's contrasts with LBYL (look before you
leap).
... # we will cover in more detail later. for now,
let's just move on.
...


>>> # if a function has no return statement, it
returns None.
>>> def print_only(name):
...     print(f'hello {name}')
...
>>> a = print_only('John')
hello John
>>> a
```

```
>>> type(a)
<class 'NoneType'>
>>> a == None
True
>>> # NoneType is a type. this type only has one
valid value, which is None.
>>> # None is similar to null, nil, or NULL in other
languages
...


>>> # handle exception
...
>>> # let's build a function that gets input and does
division.
...
>>> def do_division():
...     line1 = None
...     while(True):
...         line1 = input('give me an X:')
...         line2 = input('give me a Y:')
...         if line1 == '' or line2 == '':
...             print('done')    # enter empty value
to exit
...             break
...         result = float(line1) / float(line2)
...         print(f'result: {result}')
...
>>> do_division()
give me an X:10
give me a Y:2
result: 5.0
give me an X:11
```

```
give me a Y:2
result: 5.5
give me an X:11
give me a Y:0
Traceback (most recent call last):
 File "<stdin>", line 1, in <module>
 File "<stdin>", line 9, in do_division
ZeroDivisionError: float division by zero
>>> # it crashed if X is divided by zero.
... # let's catch the excpetion and make it more user
friendly.
...
>>> def do_division():
...     line1 = None
...     while(True):
...         line1 = input('give me an X:')
...         line2 = input('give me a Y:')
...         if line1 == '' or line2 == '':
...             print('done')    # enter empty value
to exit
...             break
...         try:
...             result = float(line1) / float(line2)
...             print(f'result: {result}')
...         except ZeroDivisionError:
...             print('cannot divided by zero')
...             continue
...
>>> do_division()
give me an X:11
give me a Y:0
cannot divided by zero
give me an X:
```

```
give me a Y:
done
>>> # what if given input other than a valid number?
...
>>> do_division()
give me an X:abc
give me a Y:def
Traceback (most recent call last):
 File "<stdin>", line 1, in <module>
 File "<stdin>", line 10, in do_division
ValueError: could not convert string to float: 'abc'
>>> # there could be all kinds of exceptions when you
taking in user input.
... # if you don't need to provide special prompt for
each error,
... # you can do a catch-all.
...
>>> def do_division():
...        line1 = None
...        while(True):
...            line1 = input('give me an X:')
...            line2 = input('give me a Y:')
...            if line1 == '' or line2 == '':
...                print('done')     # enter empty value
to exit
...                break
...            try:
...                result = float(line1) / float(line2)
...                print(f'result: {result}')
...            except Exception:     # catch all
...                print('something went wrong, try
again.')
...                continue
```

```
...
>>> do_division()
give me an X:abc
give me a Y:def
something went wrong, try again.
give me an X:!@#$
give me a Y:0
something went wrong, try again.
give me an X:
give me a Y:
done


>>> # raise your own exception
...
>>> def print_certificate(name, score):
...     if score < 50:
...         raise Exception('cannot print cert. score
too low!')
...     print(f'Congrats! {name} scored {score}.
passed!')
...
>>> print_certificate('John', 95)
Congrats! John scored 95. passed!
>>> print_certificate('Joe', 45)
Traceback (most recent call last):
 File "<stdin>", line 1, in <module>
 File "<stdin>", line 3, in print_certificate
Exception: cannot print cert. score too low!


>>> # Object Oriented Programming
...
```

```
>>> # similar to many other languages, Python is also
an OOP language.
...
>>> class Employee:
...     def __init__(self, name, department):
...         self.name = name
...         self.department = department
...
>>> e1 = Employee('John', 'Finance')
>>> print(e1)
<__main__.Employee object at 0x1068c49b0>
>>> # that doesn't give a lot of insights into the e1
object
... # __str__() is here to help.
...
>>> class Employee:
...     def __init__(self, name, department):
...         self.name = name
...         self.department = department
...     def __str__(self):
...         return f'{self.name} works for
{self.department}'
...
>>> e1 = Employee('John', 'Finance')
>>> print(e1)
John works for Finance
>>>
>>> # for any Python object, there are special
methods like __init__() and __str__().
... # you can define them for your classes.
...
>>> # class can have methods
...
```

```
>>> class Employee:
...     def __init__(self, name, department):
...         self.name = name
...         self.department = department
...     def __str__(self):
...         return f'{self.name} works for
{self.department}'
...
...     # class method, i.e., use without
instantiating an object
...     @classmethod
...     def show_company_name(cls):    # 'cls' param
is required for class methods
...         print('Acme Corporation')
...
...     def show_department_name(self):    # 'self'
is required for instance method
...         print(self.department)
...
>>> Employee.show_company_name()
Acme Corporation
>>> Employee.show_department_name()
Traceback (most recent call last):
 File "<stdin>", line 1, in <module>
TypeError: show_department_name() missing 1 required
positional argument: 'self'
>>> e1 = Employee('John', 'Finance')
>>> e1.show_department_name()
Finance


>>> # Python inheritance works similar to other
languages
```

```
...
>>> class Manager(Employee):
...     def __init__(self, name, department,
num_reports):
...         super().__init__(name, department)     #
calls __init__() of the superclass
...         self.num_reports = num_reports
...     def __str__(self):
...         return f'{self.name} heads
{self.num_reports} people in {self.department}'
...
>>> mngr = Manager('Joe', 'Finance', 6)
>>> print(mngr)
Joe heads 6 people in Finance


>>> # import library
...
>>> sin(0)
Traceback (most recent call last):
 File "<stdin>", line 1, in <module>
NameError: name 'sin' is not defined
>>> # Python has a math lib (or 'module' in Python's
language)
...
>>> import math
>>> math.sin(0)
0.0
>>> math.sin(math.pi/2)     # pi is a constant from a
module
1.0
>>>
>>> sin(pi/2)
```

```
Traceback (most recent call last):
  File "<stdin>", line 1, in <module>
NameError: name 'sin' is not defined
>>> # cannot use methods/constants directly, unless
you...
... from math import sin, pi    # to include
everything, use "from math import *"
>>> sin(pi/2)
1.0
>>> # math is a module shipped with python.
... # you can find millions of other libraries on
pypi.org.


>>> # when we introduced for loop earlier, we have
seen iterators.
... # for loop loops on a iterator.
...
>>> rainbow =
['red','orange','yellow','green','blue','indigo','vio
let']
>>> for color in rainbow:
...     print(color)
...
red
orange
yellow
green
blue
indigo
violet
>>> # that is the same as
...
```

```
>>> i = iter(rainbow)
>>> print(next(i))
red
>>> print(next(i))
orange
>>> print(next(i))
yellow
>>> print(next(i))
green
>>> print(next(i))
blue
>>> print(next(i))
indigo
>>> print(next(i))
violet
>>>
>>> # list, tuple, set, etc. are all iterables.
... # all iterables have __iter__() and __next__()
implemented.
... # when we have gone through the last iteration
and call next(),
... # it will raise a StopIteration error, which you
may catch and do something.
...
>>> print(next(i))
Traceback (most recent call last):
  File "<stdin>", line 1, in <module>
StopIteration
```

```python
>>> # Python has many handy "tricks" that you don't
easily find in other languages.
...
>>> # Reverse a string
... x = '0123456789'
>>> y = x[::-1]     # step by one but going backward
>>> y
'9876543210'


>>> # repeating, quick way to initialize variables
... x = 'a' * 10
>>> x
'aaaaaaaaaa'
>>> y = [0] * 10
>>> y
[0, 0, 0, 0, 0, 0, 0, 0, 0, 0]


>>> # multiple assignment
...
>>> x, y, z = 1, 2, 3
>>> x
1
>>> y
2
>>> z
3


>>> # same value assignment
...
>>> x = y = z = 100
```

```
>>> x
100
>>> y
100
>>> z
100


>>> # chaining comparison operations
...
>>> percent = 70
>>> if 25 < percent < 75:
...     print('mid')
...
mid


>>> # Tuple unpacking
...
>>> response = (400, 'Bad Request')
>>> code, description = response
>>> code
400
>>> description
'Bad Request'
>>>
>>> # could be used to return from a function
... def call_api():
...     # do somthing...and succeeded
...     return (200, 'OK')
...
>>> code, description = call_api()
>>> print(f'getting {description} back from server')
```

getting OK back from server

```
>>> # there are also things that may surprise you if
you came from other languages
...
>>> # be careful of what is passed in bool()
... # if it's a str, only empty str '' is False. that
means...
...
>>> bool('')
False
>>> bool('False')
True


>>> # be careful when comparing float values. they
are just approximations.
...
>>> x = 1.23
>>> x + 1.0 == 2.23
True
>>> # you thought it works, until...
...
>>> y = 1.22
>>> y + 1.0 == 2.22
False
>>> # what?!...here is why.
...
>>> (y + 1.0).as_integer_ratio()
```

```
(2499497793190625, 1125899906842624)
>>> # Python uses 2499497793190625 / 1125899906842624
to "closely" represent it.
>>> 2499497793190625 / 1125899906842624
2.219999999999998
>>> 2.22.as_integer_ratio()
(4998995586381251, 2251799813685248)
>>> # but uses 4998995586381251 / 2251799813685248 to
"closely" represent 2.22
>>> 4998995586381251 / 2251799813685248
2.22
>>> # that's why you got False when comparing them.
... # but for the first example, you are just lucky.
... # they happen to be the same within the
precision.
...
>>> (x + 1.0).as_integer_ratio()
(5021513584518103, 2251799813685248)
>>> 2.23.as_integer_ratio()
(5021513584518103, 2251799813685248)
>>>
>>> # so how to best compare float? use isclose()
from the math module.
...
>>> import math
>>> math.isclose(y + 1.0, 2.22)    # default is
comparing up to 9 decimal digits
True


>>> # EAFP (easier to ask for forgiveness than
permission) vs.
... # LBYL (look before you leap)
```

```
...     # EAFP is considered more pythonic. in other
words,
...     # do work -> if exception thrown -> catch and
handle if needed
...
>>> # in most other languages, we do LBYL like this
...
>>> person = {'name':'John', 'age':35,
'employed':True}
>>> if 'age' in person:
...         age = person['age']
... else:
...         raise Exception('age is missing')
...
>>> # in Python, EAFP
...
>>> age = person['age']
>>>
>>> # if you really want to do something else when
error happens, use 'try'
...
>>> try:
...         age = person['age']
... except KeyError:
...         # do something else...
...         raise     # re-throwing the same error
>>>
>>> # in other languages, Exceptions are expensive,
...     # and using try...catch to control flow is
discouraged.
...     # but Python makes sure throwing exceptions has
negligible performance impact,
```

```
... # and totally okay to use try to control flow as
a style.
...


>>> # Python has no switch statement
...
>>> # in other languages, you do something like this,
... #
... # var name = ''
... # var num = 3
... # switch(num) {
... #     case 1: name = 'red'; break;
... #     case 2: name = 'yellow'; break;
... #     case 3: name = 'blue'; break;
... #     default: name = 'unknown color';
... # }
... #
... # in Python, we use dict to do it.
... num = 3
>>> switcher = {1:'red', 2:'yellow', 3:'blue'}
>>> switcher.get(num, 'unknown color')
'blue'


>>> # values() method of dict returns view object,
not a list
...
>>> person = {'name':'John', 'age':35,
'employed':True}
>>> x = person.values()
>>> x
dict_values(['John', 35, True])
```

```
>>> type(x)      # not a list, but a dict_values (view)
object
<class 'dict_values'>
>>>
>>> # a view object is like a window back to the
dict,
... # when the dict is updated, the view object
follows.
... person['name'] = 'Joe'
>>> x
dict_values(['Joe', 35, True])



>>> # don't use mutable value as function parameter
default
...
>>> def make_rainbow(
...      colors =
['red','orange','yellow','green','blue','indigo','vio
let'],
...      additional_colors = []):
...      colors.extend(additional_colors)
...      # make the rainbow...
...      print(f'{len(colors)}-color rainbow')
...
>>> # make a default 7-color rainbow
... make_rainbow()
7-color rainbow
>>>
>>> # make a mega 10-color rainbow
...
make_rainbow(additional_colors=['white','gray','black
'])
```

```
10-color rainbow
>>>
>>> # make a default 7-color rainbow again, but...
... make_rainbow()
10-color rainbow
>>>
>>> # in Python, default arguments are evaluated once
when the function is defined,
... # not each time the function is called.
... # still remember that list is mutable? that
means,
... # color has 7 elements by default when function
is defined,
... # then it stays 7 colors when first time we
make_rainbow(),
... # then it becomes 10 colors when we add 3 more
colors to make the mega rainbow,
... # then it stays 10 colors when the 3rd time we
make rainbow.
...
>>> # so what is the best practice to default the
rainbow colors?
...
>>> def make_rainbow_v2(colors = None,
additional_colors = None):
...      # default it
...      if colors is None:
...          colors =
['red','orange','yellow','green','blue','indigo','vio
let']
...      if additional_colors is None:
...          additional_colors = []
...      # make the rainbow...
```

```
...         colors.extend(additional_colors)
...         # make the rainbow...
...         print(f'{len(colors)}-color rainbow')
...
>>> # make a default 7-color rainbow
... make_rainbow_v2()
7-color rainbow
>>>
>>> # make a mega 10-color rainbow
...
make_rainbow_v2(additional_colors=['white','gray','bl
ack'])
10-color rainbow
>>>
>>> # make a default 7-color rainbow again, this
time, YES!...
... make_rainbow_v2()
7-color rainbow
>>>
>>> # other than list, you may want to watch out
dict, set, etc.
>>> # those are mutable objects as well.
>>> # but using immutable objects, such as tuple,
string, etc.
>>> # as parameter defaults is totally fine.




>>> # alright, that should be enough to get you
started.
... # start USING Python!
... # using it asap is the best way to learn.
```

```
...
>>>
>>> # as next steps, learn these
... # - virtual environments
... # - packages
... # - context manager
... # - *args and **kwargs
... # - lambda
... # - duck-typing
... # - etc.
...
>>> # have fun!
...
>>> exit()
```